Also by D. P. Johnson

Beholding Transformation
Enjoying a Relationship with Jesus

Reflecting the Rabbi
Walking with Jesus

Mystery and Wonder
Loving and Living the Truth

Endorsements

D. P. Johnson is a gifted writer with a rich background in Christian ministry.
> **Louise Barnard Director of Academic Affairs,**
> Adjunct Professor of Christian Education Asia Biblical Theological Seminary of Cornerstone University

As society exerts increasing pressure on Christians to separate faith and science, fact and value, the need has never been greater for a purposeful integration of the biblical worldview with every area of learning. With wonderful acuity and practical wisdom, D. P. Johnson moves educators beyond the false dualisms of our culture by advancing a vision for education where God is the foundation, reason, and goal of all teaching and learning. This book is an invaluable resource for Christian educators who desire not only the effective transmission of information, but also the powerful transformation of students.
> **James A. Blumenstock, B.A., M.Div., Th.M., Ph.D. cand.**
> Dean of Asia Biblical Theological Seminary,
> Cornerstone University

The image of biblical integration being like threads in a Turkish rug was so powerful for me that it has caused a paradigm shift in how I share God's truth, and Christ's richness and hope, with those around me. This book will be a key tool in understanding how to integrate Truth biblically. It is an important read and will help Christian educators more fully share His Truth and worldview.
> **Pete Simano**
> Vice President for Leadership Development
> Network of International Christian Schools

Good instructors are able to communicate information clearly. However, true teachers not only develop their pupils' appetites for learning but also equip them to feed themselves. D. P. Johnson is a genuine teacher who fosters a hunger for God's Word and gives us tools for lifelong learning. In *Truth Weaving,* he both stretches us as learners and encourages us to become real teachers; objectives we should all aspire to.

John Kennedy Tannous, MD
Medical Director, Sanford International Pediatric Clinic
Professor, Sanford School of Medicine (Univ. of S. Dakota)

There is no more important subject we teach than that of God's word. This is especially true today, in an age where young people are leaving the church in unprecedented numbers. It is imperative that we reach the next generation with the timeless truth of Scripture and instill within them a strong and well-crafted worldview centered on Christ. This is just what D. P. Johnson assists teachers in doing with his book, *Truth Weaving.* Easy to digest and powerful to apply, *Truth Weaving* is a tool that should be in every Christian teacher's toolbox.

Ross Campbell
Director, OASIS International School, Ankara, Turkey

Biblical integration can be a difficult concept to understand and even more difficult to master. D. P. Johnson brings clarity and understanding in his book, *Truth Weaving.* He communicates in such a way that benefits both the novice and the experienced practitioner. Yearly he presents this topic at our teacher orientation.

Marina Lytle, Ed.S
Director, Kunming International Academy

When I first began serving in Christian schools I often heard the phrase "Biblical integration" but had absolutely no idea what it was or how to do it. Over the years, I attended conferences and purchased programs that were supposed to answer the questions of what Biblical integration was and how effectively to implement it in my school. The prescribed integration programs that I found often frustrated me. They did not address what I always believed was central to Biblical integration. D. P. Johnson does a fantastic job of capturing the real heart of Biblical integration, weaving the natural outflow of a growing relationship with Christ in your class. This book is a must-read for any Christian educator who truly wants to integrate the Bible in their classroom.

G. Duane Jobe, Ed. D.
Director, West Nairobi School, Kenya

In *Truth Weaving*, D. P. Johnson skillfully inspires Christian educators to build their lives and teaching on the firm foundation of Jesus Christ and engage their students in the *truth-seeking* process.

Lydia M. Zuidema, Ed.S
Director of Academic Development
Network of International Christian Schools

Every teacher, regardless of the discipline they teach, should integrate Bible into their curriculum. Teachers need to make God relevant in everything. This book by D. P. Johnson will equip the reader with tools to integrate the Bible effectively throughout the curriculum. Go and Teach the TRUTH!

Rex Freel
Director, International Christian School,
Uijongbu, South Korea

Truth Weaving

Truth Weaving
Biblical Integration for God's Glory and Their Abundant Living

D. P. Johnson

Waking Elms Press

Cover photo: Detail of a handwoven antique carpet from Taspinar, Aksaray Province, Turkey

Contact the author:
Waking.Elms@gmail.com

Waking Elms Press

ISBN-13: 978-0692455401
ISBN-10: 069245540X

TO MY FAMILY

Contents

An Invitation

Come have a cup of coffee with me. Let us take a break from the busyness of life, settle into comfortable chairs and talk about our role as teachers. It is a high and holy calling. Christ has entrusted us with the work of the kingdom. Whether we teach algebra, chemistry or literature, the Master Teacher has called us to this task for kingdom purposes; purposes which are even greater and larger than achieving success in the classroom.

Our calling is to be weavers of truth, and biblical integration is how we do this. I invite you to join me in exploring this important topic. We will discuss eight central questions as we learn the techniques of truth weaving:

What is the first principle for those who desire to integrate the Bible?

What is biblical integration?

Why should we integrate the Bible into our lessons?

What is essential for weaving vivid integration?

How do we weave the essentials into biblically integrated lessons?

How can we sharpen and use our own unique methods to weave powerful integration?

How do we integrate for non-Christian students and in non-Christian settings?

How can we begin in a way that will ensure our future success?

Come. Pull up your chair and have this conversation with me. I pray it will provide practical answers that will enable you to create vivid and powerful truth weavings. It is time to change the way our students see things. It is time to change the way our students live.

Conversation 1: First Things First

Of Tractors and Men

I started operating heavy machinery at the age of eleven. The *Massey Ferguson 245* is small, as tractors go, but its back tire stood taller than I did when I started driving. I beamed as I drove around the field tedding alfalfa.

One day I was responsible for an extra-large field. "Be sure you watch the gage. You'll need to add fuel before you're done," Dad said as he dropped off a can of diesel. The novelty of tractor work had not worn off yet. It was a beautiful Vermont summer day, and I loved being trusted with such a big responsibility. I was so careful. I wanted to be sure to ted every bit of the half-dried alfalfa.

Three-fourths of the way through, it happened. The tractor gave a shuddering jerk, let out a sigh and stopped dead. At first, I thought I hit something. I didn't. I could not figure out what was wrong. Then I remembered. The diesel! I forgot to pay attention to the gage. It was empty, and I sighed with relief. It was an easy problem to fix, or so I thought.

I ran to the edge of the field and lugged the heavy can back to the tractor. After putting the fuel in, I tried to start it. It still would not turn over. I tried and tried. Finally, I faced the fact. I needed Dad.

I found him and said that the tractor wouldn't start. "Is there diesel in the tank?" was his first question.

"Yes," I replied. I was quite proud I had solved that problem on my own. "After it stopped, I filled it up, but now it won't start again."

"Did you run it dry?"

"Yes, but it's full now." I felt like Dad was getting at something that I did not see.

"That's the problem. You can't just fill up a diesel tank once the engine's run dry."

My dad grabbed his tools and headed out to fix the tractor. I still do not know what he did, but it took him a couple of hours to get it running again.

I learned an important lesson about tractors that day.

For the next eight years of my life, I clocked hundreds of hours on various diesel tractors around our family farm. I never again ran a tractor dry. I did it to the family car once or twice when I first got my license, but that is another story.

Years later, my dad's words echoed in my mind when I went through difficult times. "You can't just fill up a diesel tank once the engine's run dry." I learned this is not just true for tractors. It is true about people, too.

We cannot run on empty. We need to keep our fuel tank full. If it goes dry, we need more than just a quick refill to get going again.

The Overflow Principle

As teachers who seek to integrate the Bible, we need to be full. This is the first principle:

Successful biblical integrators need hearts and lives filled with God's Word.

God introduces us to this important concept in his promise to Abraham:

> Now the LORD said to Abram, "Go from your country and your kindred and your father's house to the land that I will show you. And I will make of you a great nation, and I will bless you and make your name great, so that you will be a blessing. (Genesis 12.1-2).

Do you see it? "I will bless you... so that you will be a blessing." We can call this the overflow principle. God pours into our lives so that we have something to pour into the lives of others. We have nothing to give until something has been given to us. We cannot be a blessing until we have been blessed.

We also see this principle at work in 1 John 4.19. "We love because he first loved us." We love out of the overflowing abundance of God's love lavished on us.

This principle is not just in Genesis and First John. It is everywhere in Scripture. God fills us with His love and blessings so that we can pour them out in acts of love toward Him and our brothers and sisters.

God's love and blessing is a gift He gives as we enter into His presence. We have the privilege of listening to Him and feasting on His Word. In our time with Him, He enlarges us and fills our increase. This filling is relational, not mechanical. It is a relationship of friendship and real interaction.

Jesus' transfiguration was a defining moment for His inner circle of disciples. In His presence, they saw Him as He really was. The Father spoke to tell them what they must do. He said, "This is my beloved son; listen to him." (Mark 9.7). Listening is the central task for all disciples.[1]

We are to listen like banqueters dining with a friend. God invites His servants to feast on His word (Ezekiel 3.1-3, Jeremiah 15.16 and Revelation 10.9-10). Daily we need sustenance from the milk and meat of Scripture. Without it, we will be weak and unprepared to share the truth, love and blessings that God offers.

We are to serve out of the overflow of the riches God daily gives to us. We cannot pass on a blessing that we have not experienced. We can only lead people to places in which we ourselves dwell. God generously shares His love and blessing. From His bountiful overflow, we serve.

Conversation 2: A Definition

Turkish Rugs

Our two-year-old daughter took one look at our new Turkish apartment and shrieked with joy. She loved to run, and the long hallway gave her the runway she needed. As she took off down the hall, we knew it was only a matter of time before she would slip and hit her head on the bare, slippery, unforgiving tiles.

On the second day in our new home, we encountered another problem. Our downstairs neighbor came up. "I can't stand that pitter-patter of 'little witch' steps. They echo through our ceiling. Control you daughter!" she demanded. "I expect silence and peace of mind when I'm in my home. Do something."

We consulted our friends who were helping us settle in. They immediately knew what to do. "Let's go rug shopping," they suggested. I did not see the connection. "Rugs cover the slippery tiles and dampen the sound," they explained.

The Ulus quarter of Ankara, Turkey, quite possibly, has the best bargains on rugs west of Persia. We wound through narrow alleys clogged with people, peddlers and dust. It was high summer and the smell of dust mixed with sweat and spices as we pressed up against absolute strangers.

We found the right door and descended through a maze of basement-level shops. Our friend found the one he was looking for. "Used Turkish rugs, cheap," seemed to be the owner's mantra.

They were beautiful, but I knew nothing about them. The shopkeeper poured us Turkish tea in short tulip-shaped glasses as he explained what makes a good rug. I learned to recognize the difference between machine and handwoven rugs. I learned that a good handmade rug could last for generations. My friend showed me how to count the number of threads in a thumb width. More is better. The shopkeeper was not in a hurry. He poured us more tea, then showed us different types of patterns and explained the degree of difficulty in weaving each one.

In the end, we settled on some relatively inexpensive machine-made wool rugs. I told the shop owner we hoped to come back to examine his handwoven beauties in the future.

What Is Biblical Integration?

Biblical integration is a hot topic in Christian education. Because it is familiar, it often slips into conversation without a definition. The first rule of logic insists we define our terms, especially if they are common concepts open to a number of interpretations. The definition that we will be using is as follows:

Biblical integration is weaving the biblical worldview into the subject and lives of students.

The act of weaving involves interlacing multiple threads together so that they form one unified whole. A weaver makes a Turkish carpet with thousands of individual threads in a host of colors. Each is deliberately chosen and carefully placed. Each has a role and is necessary. Once the weaver is finished, removing even a single thread will damage the whole. The many now function as one.

A biblically integrated lesson is like that. It is a complex weaving of the subject and biblical content. The teacher-weaver chooses the colors and the patterns for each lesson.

As we weave a carpet-lesson, one type of thread is the biblical content. In any given lesson, there may be many or few of them. Another type of thread is the subject matter. Again, the amount depends on the purposes of the teacher-weaver.

One carpet may be primarily green, while another may have just a touch to highlight an aspect of the pattern. That is the way it is with biblical integration. One lesson may contain a great deal of biblical content, while another has just a trace. Both are biblical integration because the subject content interweaves with biblical truth. Both have a place in our curriculum.

Biblical Integration is Not a Bulletin Board

I have a bulletin board in my classroom. I tack notes and student work on it. Currently I have a sketch of a four-faced cherub an eighth grader drew after reading the first chapter of Ezekiel. I can add another sketch or two to the bulletin board but it will not really affect the board. The angel sketch is impressive and noticeable, but it does not really do anything to the board except make a small hole where the tack went in. I can remove the picture and the board itself is unaffected.

Much of so-called biblical integration is like this. We tack an illustration or verse onto a lesson and call it integration. It is not. Integration is not just something we tack on. To be integration, it has to be woven into the fabric of the lesson.

The Test

There is a simple test for integration. If we remove the biblical content, does the lesson unravel or fall apart? If the lesson is intact when we remove the Biblical content, it was not integration. The lesson was serving as a bulletin board.

This is not to say that tacking a Bible verse onto our lessons is a bad thing. It can be good, important and the right thing to do, but it is not biblical integration.

Christianity is both objectively true and subjectively experienced. In biblical integration, we cannot ignore either! Without content, Christianity is vague warm feelings. If we ignore the subjective experience of living out the biblical content, we are just teaching an encyclopedia of esoteric facts.

The Bible is central. It unifies the objective and subjective. It is the foundation for our subjective feelings and right understanding of God and reality. Even in an unfallen state, Adam needed the Word of God.

I could not teach calculus. I do not know the content well enough. In the same way, if we do not know the Bible's truth claims, we will be unable to integrate them into our lesson content. Lack of biblical knowledge is one of the main reasons we have difficulty integrating the Bible. We could all know scripture better. We need to do something more than "read a chapter a day to keep the devil away."

Worldview Formation

Worldview formation is the focus of biblical integration. A worldview is simply one's way of viewing the world, the whole world. It provides an all-encompassing approach to understanding reality. Francis Schaffer begins his excellent book, *A Christian Manifesto*, with this statement, "The basic problem of the Christians... is that they have seen things in bits and pieces instead of totals."[2] We weave the Bible into our subject so that our students can develop a comprehensive worldview built on the truth of God's Word.

Worldview Glasses

A worldview is the pair of glasses through which we see the world. Having an inaccurate worldview is like wearing the wrong prescription. Some things might seem clear enough, but others are blurry and out of focus.

Our work as biblical integrators is to help others find the right prescription. It is like the work of *New Eyes for the Needy*. This non-profit organization helps the underprivileged see the world clearly. They collect used prescription eyeglasses and distribute them to those who need them most.[3]

We live in a needy time. So few have a biblical worldview. So few can see clearly. *Christianity Today*, reporting on a survey by the *Barna Research Group*, stated that only nine percent of Americans have a biblical worldview. Even more sobering for those of us who educate the young is Barna's statistic about young adults. Only one-half of one percent (0.5%) of eighteen to twenty-three-year-olds has a biblical worldview.[4] While the study was limited to the United States, we can assume a similar percentage in other post-Christian nations.

What does it mean to have a biblical worldview? How we answer this question is important. Our answer determines our task as integrators. When a person has a biblical worldview, it means that they see the world through the lens of God's Word. We all need glasses. We are sinful people living in a sinful word. Sin corrupts our sight. We desperately need the right prescription to help us see. Our work as biblical integrators is essential.

Worldview Hypothesis and Content

Freud's definition of a worldview is the best that I have encountered. A worldview is "an intellectual construction which solves all the problems of our existence uniformly on the basis of one overriding hypothesis, which, accordingly, leaves no question unanswered and in which everything that interests us finds its fixed place."[5]

Freud rightly places a hypothesis at the center of a worldview. A hypothesis is a starting point for attempting to make sense of the data, but we can and should test that starting point.

We state the hypothesis of a Biblical worldview as follows:

God exists and has revealed Himself and His truth in His word and works.

We identify several important components of our hypothesis. God exists. Truth exists. We can know God and truth. God's revelation is in a format we can understand; He fit it to our faculties. He has taken the initiative, and He desires us to know Him and His truth. Therefore, our searching is a response to God. Questioning and seeking truth is good.

Our hypothesis also tells us that there are two sources of revelation. Both His word and His works reveal Him. The word of God is, first and foremost, the living Word, Jesus Christ, God the Son. It is also the spoken word of the Bible, delivered by the living Word through the inspiration of the Spirit. God has also revealed Himself and truth through His works, beginning with creation and including the entirety of all His actions – past, present and future. The two vehicles of revelation are not equal, but they are in harmony.

A worldview begins with a central hypothesis and then proceeds from that starting point to answer a number of important questions:

1. Who is God?
2. What is real?
3. Who am I, and what is my relationship to others?
4. What is good, and how can I be good?
5. What is true, and how do I know it?
6. Why am I here?

The final question, the why, or purpose question, pulls them all together and articulates the implications of the other answers. This question is so important and so connected to the others that we could use it to evaluate the whole worldview.

Based on these questions, we can identify six major worldview categories.[6] Different organizational schemes are possible, but these six seem to find the perfect balance of being specific but not overwhelming in number. We can use these categories to express any worldview:

1. God (Theology)
2. Reality (Metaphysics)
3. Humanity and Community (Anthropology and Sociology)
4. Values and Ethics (Axiology)
5. Knowledge and Truth (Epistemology)
6. Meaning and Purpose (Teleology)

The Power of Stories

A story is the best way to express the biblical worldview. It can be (and often is) expressed in other ways, but God delivered it to us as a story. Consider this example: God did not present one of the most pivotal moments in the Bible, the fall into sin, as a set of abstract theological propositions. Instead, He told the story of how it happened.

Years ago, I read that more than eighty percent of Bible is story. I do not remember the source, but the statistic has deeply affected how I teach. Narrative also frames many of the non-story parts of the Bible. We understand the Sermon on the Mountain (Matthew 5-7) and Olivet Discourse (Matthew 24-25) within the context of the story of Jesus' life and ministry. Paul's life story presented in Acts is the setting in which we interpret his epistles.

Why so many stories? Simple. Stories are powerful! We remember stories. They are almost magical. We can observe their power in any given church service. We have all seen it before. The pastor drones on, and our attention wanders. Then it happens. He says the magic words. They sound something like this: "A strange thing happened to me when I was washing the windows yesterday." Suddenly everyone is paying attention. Window washing is not exciting, but we know we are in for a story, and we want to hear it.

The Biblical Worldview Story

God wired us to love stories, and His Word is the grandest story of all.

Each story, no matter how simple or complex, has three basic parts: (1) the setting, (2) the problem and (3) the solution. The biblical story is no exception. These three elements tell the biblical worldview simply and concisely. They provide meaning and direction for our existence:

1. Setting: Creation, perfection and original purpose
2. Problem: Rebellion and the distortion of original purpose
3. Solution (in two parts): Redemption and restoration of original purpose (centered on the incarnation, life,

death and resurrection of Jesus and consummated at
His return)

In the beginning, God created everything and it was
very good. Adam and Eve rebelled against God and
alienated themselves from Him. At the perfect time in
history, God sent His Son. He became a human being,
lived a sinless life, died in the place of sinners and
resurrected on the third day for the redemption of His
people. He is at work restoring all things. At the
appointed time, He will return and dwell with His people
forever.

This story explains the origin and original purpose of
all things. It shows us that things are distorted and are
not the way they should be. It explains that redemption,
or rescue, is only possible because of the incarnation, life,
death and resurrection of Jesus Christ. It shows us that
restoration is in process, yet certain. The consummation
will be at Christ's return, and He will usher in a new
creation.

The story explains the past, present and future of our
universe. It shows us where we have been, where we are
and where we are going. It teaches us the source of
healing and invites us into relationship with God. It gives
us meaning, purpose and a task to accomplish.

The story teaches us to ask four questions as we seek
to integrate the biblical worldview. We can ask these
questions about any object or activity:

1. How did God intend it to be?
2. How do we distort, misuse or misunderstand it?

3. How does Jesus (in His teaching, life, death and resurrection) redeem and restore it to its God-intended purpose? How does He involve us in this work?

4. What will it look like when Jesus returns and brings about full restoration?

The first question concerns the **setting**. What was each thing's original place and purpose? How did God intend it to be in His sinless creation? We primarily look to the creation narratives to discover our answers.

The second question examines the **problem**—how our rebellion and sin has affected God's good world. How have we distorted, misused or misunderstood it? This world does not currently operate according to God's original intention. We, in our sin, have defaced God's good creation. In our sin and rebellion, we seek to build lives and belief systems apart from God. At this step, we examine non-biblical worldviews that offer competing answers to our questions. These worldviews distort, misuse or misunderstand reality.

The third and fourth questions concern the **solution**. The two are united, but we can separate them for detailed examination. Jesus brings redemption to all of creation by His incarnation—His teaching, life, death and resurrection. He accomplished this redemption on the cross. When He said it was finished, it was. However, there is also an ongoing process of restoration. It will not reach its consummation until He returns. Redemption and restoration are about restoring and experiencing right relationships with God, self, others and creation.

The work of restoration is His, yet He invites His people to participate with Him in it. Restoration occurs when we follow God's commands and return to His designs and purposes. He designed everything in all creation for His glory and our abundant living. In the work of restoration, our Savior and Lord is our guide, model and enabler (through His gift of the Holy Spirit).

We are to collaborate with Jesus in this work of restoration until He returns. At the consummation of all things, He will bring full restoration and perfect the work He began at His first coming. We, His people, will dwell with Him forever in a new heaven and earth.

Weaving Trigonometry into the Biblical Story

The story approach opens up integration to new vistas. Take math, for example. It is one of the most difficult subjects to integrate. Because of this difficulty, we often resort to lame, flat integrations such as "a triangle is a way to help us understand the trinity."

Instead, consider this integration of biblical restoration and trigonometry; God calls the redeemed to collaborate with Him to bring His love and gospel to a needy world. Trigonometry is necessary to build a stable house. This advanced math is what we need to demonstrate God's love to the destitute. When we know trigonometry and can apply it to the building of homes, we need not send the homeless away with an empty blessing of "Be warm and filled." (James 2.16). Even greater integration is possible if we go out and build!

The Subject and Life

All of life and reality is within God's story, so we need to see *everything* from His point of view. To understand

every aspect of the world through the lens of Scripture—
this is a Biblical worldview. Every subject needs biblical
integration, even those that are not traditionally school
subjects. Nothing is outside the scope of the biblical
worldview.

Successful biblical integration connects God's truth to
life. It changes the way we see things and the way we live.

An Example: Natural Resources

The following example is certainly not complete or
exhaustive, but it serves to illustrate the process of
applying the biblical story to the topic of natural
resources.

1. *How did God intend it to be?*

    The world's natural resources are God's
    creation, which He called very good (Genesis 1).
    He entrusted these natural resources to the
    stewardship of the human race (Genesis 2). A
    steward is one who cares for goods that belong to
    another. The parable in Matthew 25.14-30
    illustrates the stewardship principle. In this story,
    the master entrusts three servants with an
    amount of money. Two are good stewards who
    use it well; one is not. While the context is not
    specifically about natural resources, it does
    illustrate the seriousness of good stewardship.

2. *How do we distort, misuse or misunderstand it?*
    (How do non-biblical, competing worldviews
    distort, misuse or misunderstand it?)

    Due to our sin, our relationship with God and
    His creation is not what it should be. Currently,
    nature is groaning under the curse and eagerly

awaiting the revelation of the children of God (Romans 8.19-22). We distort natural resources and their use, primarily in two ways. Some people deify nature and serve the creation rather than the Creator (Romans 1.25). Others exploit and misuse natural resources to satisfy their own selfish desires and greedy pursuits. Both actions are idolatry (Colossians 3.5).

3. *How does Jesus (in His teaching, life, death and resurrection) redeem and restore it to its God-intended purpose? How does He involve us in this work?*

Jesus' life illustrates the proper use of natural resources. He is our model of right stewardship. He redeems us so that we may be in right relationship with God and His creation. When we recognize the rightful place of God, we can also recognize the rightful place of His creation. As redeemed people, we are no longer slaves to sin. We are free and need not relate to the world and others with greed and selfishness. We are free to be like Christ in all aspects of life, including stewardship. We see His refusal to waste resources in the command to pick up the leftover pieces of bread after the feeding of the 5,000. As a steward, He also used the Spirit's resources to serve, obey and glorify God. We can recognize creation as ultimately belonging to God and treat it as our Lord's property, neither deifying it nor foolishly squandering it on our greed. Like good and faithful stewards, we can work it and invest it so that we glorify our Master by the good return we earn on what He has entrusted to us.

4. *What will it look like when Jesus returns and brings about full restoration?*

One day we will stand face-to-face with our Master. If we have served in obedience, He will say, "Well done, my good and faithful servant. You have been faithful over a little; I will set you over much. Enter into the joy of your master." (Matthew 25.21). Jesus will one day complete his work of making all things new. He will reign as king over a new, restored creation (Revelation 19-22).

Conversation 3: Why?

Why Ask Questions?

What is the primary task of the teacher? I love questions like this. They just beg for examination and discussion. Sitting in the sun on a breezy fall day with a steaming cup of coffee and discussing meaningful questions with friends is one of life's great pleasures.

I like questions and discussion so much, that most years my wife gives me a gift of them for my birthday. Either as a couple or with a few friends, we spend an evening in discussion. We each prepare a few choice questions that are sure to spark lively debate. Then we brew a pot of strong coffee and discuss them late into the night. It is always my favorite gift.

Questions are not all created equally. In the gallery of questions, masterpieces are rare. Mediocre ones are, by far, the most common. Some fall flat and lifeless. Some are misguiding and confusing. Many are simply uninteresting.

A good question is a treasure. One of my most important tasks as an educator is to kindle curiosity and get my students to ask questions and discuss them. I teach them the characteristics of a good question and make them create questions about everything. We practice until creating and asking become second nature to them.

I know I have been successful when I hear a question like this, "Why should we ask questions?" When it comes up in class, we stop and discuss it.

"Why?" is a search for purpose. Those who have purpose act, those who do not, will not. Purpose keeps us going when giving up is the easiest option. I tell my students that only those who have an answer to "Why ask questions?" will persist in asking them when the course is over and done. Answers to "why questions" give us passion and perseverance, but they must be answers we believe in.

Why Integrate?

Why should we do biblical integration? It is an important question, and I always ask it when I lead an integration workshop.

Two of the most commonly given answers are not actually answers. They are ways to dodge the question. The first is this, "It's my duty as a Christian educator." Why is it our duty? The second answerless answer is, "My principal requires it of me." Why does he or she?

We need a real answer to this question. We need an answer we believe in. Those who have one will persist in the hard work of biblical integration. Teaching is certainly easier if we choose not to integrate the Bible. So why should we do it? What is our purpose and goal?

Teachers integrate the Bible into the subject and lives of students to enable them to develop a biblical vision of life that will guide them to think and act for God's glory and their own abundant living.

A Vision of Life: A Map for Life's Journey

Let us examine our purpose statement. In our previous conversation, we talked extensively about what a worldview is. Now we emphasize why it matters. A person's worldview is their vision for life.

Life is a journey through confusing and unknown territory. A unifying vision of life provides the map a person uses for navigation. This map organizes the details of life experience into a coherent and meaningful whole. It brings clarity and focus so that life does not feel like a random, chaotic flood of experience. In order to do so, a vision for life should incorporate ALL of life and provide an organizational key for its diversity. Only when we have a unifying principle that encompasses everything, can life begin to make sense and have meaning.

Our integration teaches the students to find their life vision in the biblical worldview story of creation, fall, redemption and consummation. All their scattered experiences fit within the biblical story. Everything receives meaning from God the Creator and Redeemer.

This biblical vision for life allows us to see God and all of reality rightly. His revelation gives us the corrective lens we need so that we can see the world from His perspective. Biblical integration is worldview formation. We are not just seeking to inform the students about bits of biblical trivia. Each integration lesson is part of the overall goal of shaping an all-encompassing biblical worldview map for the student.

A unifying vision also protects the student from wrongly dividing life. A sacred/ secular dualism beckons to Christians, but it is a siren's song that shipwrecks lives. It divides God's Kingdom. It says He is sovereign King in the sacred and spiritual realm, but He has no claims beyond this.

Furthermore, a unifying vision keeps truth intact. The truth of God's word and the truth of God's works fit together. The truth of the Bible and the truth of the subject are in harmony.

Thought and Action

A life vision map provides a guide for student thought and action. Biblical integration begins in the classroom but extends its reach to include all of life. It is not just about knowing subject content. Action is the fruit of thought. The two are inseparable. Our goal is to enable students not only to know the biblical worldview but also to manifest it in their actions.

Why do some students seem to know all the right answers, but not act according to what they know? There are two reasons. First, their fruit may be small and immature, but growing. A newly formed fruit is almost invisible in the bud. The second reason for a lack of action is that the content of the biblical worldview has not permeated their thinking. It has informed but not transformed them.

Biblical thought and action sound good, right, noble and Christian, but why bother? What difference does it make? Why should students think and act biblically?

God's Glory and Our Good

We give students a unified vision for life founded on the biblical worldview story so that they can think and act biblically. We desire them to think and act biblically for God's glory and their good.

Why should they care about God's glory? First, as our infinitely good Creator and Redeemer, He is worthy. To glorify is to recognize and proclaim the weight and worth of a person or thing. To glorify is to worship. Worship encompasses all of life. A meal with friends, taking out the trash, reading a novel, a sunset walk, even studying or grading papers, all of these are worship. To view worship only as a few songs sung on a Sunday morning misses the point almost entirely.

Second, God's glory and our good go together. God created us to glorify Him. His glory is at the forefront of His purposes. "But truly, as I live... all the earth shall be filled with the glory of the LORD," (Numbers 14.21). "For the earth will be filled with the knowledge of the glory of the LORD as the waters cover the sea." (Habakkuk 2.14). "All the nations you have made shall come and worship before you, O Lord, and shall glorify your name." (Psalm 86.9). Glorifying God is not some abstract, intangible ideal.

What is an abundant life? When we glorify God with our thoughts and actions, our hearts overflow with joy and our lives become abundant, full and meaningful. What does it mean to live abundantly? To explore this, we need a biblically grounded purpose statement. It is not primarily, as many claim, about health and prosperity. Scripture's answer is much better than that.

Before any description, we need to recognize that an abundant life is a gift that comes from Christ the king. We cannot achieve it by self-effort. If we could earn it, then Jesus would not have needed to come. Abundant life is a gift that is slowly unwrapped through acts of obedience.

As it is unwrapped, we see it as a fourfold threshold to cross by grace-empowered obedience. In an abundant life, the individual: (1) cultivates meaningful relationships with God, self and others, (2) matures in identity and purpose, (3) seeks truth, beauty and goodness and (4) actively engages the world. The following vision statement expresses it:

Love, grow, seek, engage—live to the fullest for God's glory.

Taken together, thinking and acting biblically for God's glory and our abundance describe a life lived in right relationship with God. Our ultimate aim in integration is the renewal of minds for relational ends. We are not just preparing students for the classroom. We are preparing them to live well with God.

Teacher's Product or Student's Process?

Typically, we think of biblical integration as a product to deliver, but in reality, it is primarily a thinking process to practice. We model biblical integration in the classroom with the intention that our students will learn to do it for themselves.

Biblical integration *is* a product we create and present, but we cannot stop there. We want the students to learn the content of our integration products, but our end goal is always for them to learn the process and do it themselves. If all they do is learn prepackaged teacher-created products, they will not be able to feed themselves. They need to have the skill and ability to weave the Bible into all the new content they encounter.

As we learn how to do biblical integration, we also need to teach our students how to do it. When they learn to do it, they can feed themselves and others.

Conversation 4: An Introduction to the Model

Black and White TVs

When I was a child, our only television was a small black and white set my parents had received as a wedding gift. Since we lived out in the country, we only got three channels. Two were the same network, just broadcast from different cities. The only real difference between them was the six o'clock local news. Our other station was PBS, the Public Broadcasting Service. We did not turn on the TV often, but when we did, it was usually a family affair. All six of us would crowd around that thirteen-inch black and white screen to watch our favorite program, *Gilligan's Island*. Each week featured a new escape plan devised by the eclectic group of people trapped on the deserted island. They failed every time. Once when we were watching the program, a snake my brother and I had caught got free. It slithered down the stairs and dropped anaconda-like on top of the TV. My parents were not happy, and I never did find out how that episode ended.

When I was in seventh grade, our relatives thought it was time for us to enter the modern era. They bought us a color TV. *Gilligan's Island* was the first show I saw on our new set. I remember thinking it was of major significance to discover that Gilligan's shirt was red. I am not sure why it mattered, but it did. I determined right there and then that when you watch in black and white, you miss things.

After that first episode, I noticed the letters "RGB" on the bottom left corner of the television set. I asked my parents what it meant. "It's an abbreviation for red, green and blue," my mom said.

"Why?" I wanted to know. My parents explained to me the marvels of color television. They told me that all the colors the TV displayed were combinations of red, green and blue. I was fascinated. All the dozens of colors I saw on Gilligan's island were the result of mixing three colors. Amazing!

I asked about our old TV. My mom patiently explained. "A black and white TV works in a similar way, but only uses two colors. It's sort of obvious from the name, don't you think?"

Biblical Integration in Full Living Color

Biblical integration models have a lot in common with television sets. Some are black and white, and some are RGB color. Both give us the picture, but when you watch in black and white, you miss things.

Often we settle for a "shades of grey" model of biblical integration. Like a black and white TV, it only has two colors—the Bible and the subject. Such models give our students a muted picture.

We can help them experience the Bible in full living color. Biblical integration should be like an RGB TV. Such integration has three interrelated and overlapping components that come together to create a bright, vivid picture. Powerful integration requires us to be experts in three areas: (1) our academic subject, (2) the Bible and (3) our students.

Knowing Our Subject and the Bible

To begin with, powerful integration depends upon knowing our subject matter. Depth and accuracy in integration demand it. This includes knowing our unit and lesson objectives so we can teach the topic appropriately to our student audience.

Integration also requires knowledge of the Bible and the truth it teaches about our academic subjects. This can be difficult for a number of reasons. The Bible is a large and complicated book. We may lack formal training in theology and biblical interpretation. Perhaps we cannot find trustworthy resources. Maybe the topic seems remote from the biblical text, and we cannot determine what the Bible says about it. We might not even know how to start looking for answers. These, or dozens of other problems like them, confront us at this step.

Biblical integration compels us to surmount these difficulties and discover what the Bible says about our topic of instruction, but that is secondary. Our first priority is to build our own lives on the sure foundation of God's word. We need to saturate our hearts and minds with God's truth. How do we do that? How can we know

His Word so well that integrating it into the subject and lives of students becomes second nature? There is no magic bean that grows knowledge overnight. A lifetime is not enough to learn it all. The process of coming to know God and His truth is slow, like the growing of an oak, like coming to know a person. Real knowledge of biblical truth is relational rather than academic. It begins when we enter God's presence and immerse ourselves in His Word.

How do we grow in knowledge? Here are a couple of practical suggestions to help us cultivate our understanding of God and His truth:

First, go to the source. The Bible is primary. We should spend more time studying the Bible and less time in secondary sources. Sermons and books on theology are fine and have their place, but through disciplined study and the ministry of the Holy Spirit's illumination, we can discover God's hidden riches. They will be even more precious to us because we have fought for them.

Second, study the Bible by book. When God delivered His word to us, He gave it in books. Every book of the Bible instructs us in all six worldview categories, yet sometimes in our rush to know the Bible, we go, instead, for a topical approach. Topical studies are narrow and confined to select portions of Scripture. This approach is too limiting. It is ill equipped for worldview formation, because a worldview is a big picture that encompasses everything. The topical approach to study produces uneven growth. It instructs us deeply about our selected topic, but we can be completely unaware of other topics and the relationship of the parts to the whole.

There is a place for topical studies when we are weaving biblical integration lessons, but for our daily sustenance, we should most often ingest God's word as He delivered it to us—in books. *See the appendix for a list of suggested books of the Bible to start reading in order to lay a strong worldview foundation.*

As we spend time with God, reading His Word, our minds are renewed and we grow in His image and likeness. Relational knowledge is transformative. Romans 12.2 tells us that those with renewed minds and transformed lives are able to discern God's revealed will and live it out. As His truth becomes part of us, we begin to see how it connects and applies to life. Transformative Bible study always includes application, and biblical integration is a specialized form of application. It seeks to apply the text to an academic topic as well as to personal life.

Knowing Our Students

The student is the third component of biblical integration.[7] This third element is what is often lacking in many models. When it is present, it adds vibrant color. Finding ways to connect the truth to the student's life, culture and experiences is only possible if we know them. Real connection is about relationships, not formulas. We do not teach a vague universal person. We are speaking to specific individuals. Each person is a unique social, emotional, intellectual, spiritual and physical being. These five aspects create a one-of-a-kind, unrepeatable personality and experience set. As we accept our students for who they are, we can begin to know them and enter into authentic relationship.

How do we get to know our students? At the risk of stating the obvious, we develop relationships with them in the same way we come to know anyone. Talk with them, listen to them and spend time with them. Create opportunities in (and if possible, outside of) the classroom. Most teachers help students get to know each other, but it is equally important that we foster the student-teacher relationship. As we grow in knowing our students, we are able to tailor our biblical integration to their unique interests and personalities. Powerful integration does not happen in a one-size fits all approach.

Paul's methods teach us much about meaningful connection that opens doors for sharing the truth. In 1 Corinthians 9.19-23, he reveals his heart:

> For though I am free from all, I have made myself a servant to all, that I might win more of them. To the Jews I became as a Jew, in order to win Jews. To those under the law I became as one under the law (though not being myself under the law) that I might win those under the law. To those outside the law I became as one outside the law (not being outside the law of God but under the law of Christ) that I might win those outside the law. To the weak I became weak, that I might win the weak. I have become all things to all people, that by all means I might save some. I do it all for the sake of the gospel, that I may share with them in its blessings.

In Acts 17, we see this attitude in practice. Paul connected with the philosophers in Athens. As a Rabbinic Jew, the differences between him and the polytheistic philosophers might have seemed insurmountable, but Paul observed and learned the culture so he could discover points of contact. He used those points of contact to engage with them in meaningful communication. Our students live in a different culture than we do. Our differences might not be quite as significant as those of Paul and the philosophers, but close. Like Paul, we need to make ourselves students of our students.

Meaningful Communication

When we know our students, we are able to identify powerful points of contact that open the door for memorable and meaningful communication. A good point of contact will do two things for our integration. First, it facilitates understanding by illustrating our topic as an example of the truth we are teaching (either positive or negative). Second, it can also be a hook to generate interest and capture the student's imagination. Be creative. God's truth integrated into subjects and lives is not dry, dull or dusty. It is a crime to bore people with God's Word.

How do we discover good connections? As relational teachers, we can begin with three important points of contact: (1) media, (2) experiences and (3) culture and current events.

Media

The easiest entry into our students' culture is through currently popular media, such as songs, movies, television programs, games, websites, books and magazines. The songs and movies that speak to them resonate for a reason. They give voice to what is in their hearts and minds. Popular media expresses their needs, struggles, fears, frustrations, problems, longings and hopes. Media review sites can be helpful for identifying themes and content for making our connections. One of my favorite Christian review sites is hollywoodjesus.com.

Experiences

Media is good, but personal experience is better! What is popular in the media is always changing. Remember how quickly last summer's "in" song fell out of favor? We soon forget a movie, but the memory of a lived experience can last a lifetime. Use those experiences to shape powerful integration.

The teacher does not need to wait passively for events to happen. A thoughtful instructor can even *create* experiences to harvest for biblical integration. Memorable connections occur when the teacher crafts shared classroom experiences.

Culture and Current Events

There is more to a culture than media. Cross-cultural missionaries spend years learning their host culture. We need to adopt their mindset as we reach out to our students. Connecting to the students' subcultures makes the biblical content come alive for them. Among other cultural products and happenings, use current events. What school, local, national or global events are happening around us? Use them to illustrate the integration topic.

We are to know our audience and connect our teaching to it. When we use fitting connections, we are speaking our students' language.

Our model weaves together knowledge of the subject, the Bible and the students. Such integration is vivid and colorful. It brings transformation, healing and growth so that our students can experience the abundant life that God offers through Christ!

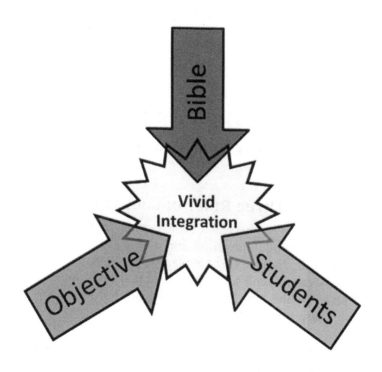

Conversation 5: A Recipe for Biblical Integration

Three Rules of Cooking

My mom is an excellent cook. People "just happen" to show up around dinnertime, and they are always invited to join in. Somehow, there is plenty of food and everyone walks away full and satisfied. I don't make it home as often as I'd like, but the food and laughter around her table is always a highlight of the trip.

Whatever she cooks is sure to be delicious, but of all the things she makes, her dinner rolls are the most famous. She says every chef needs a specialty, and the rolls are hers. The recipe is a family secret, passed down from her grandmother. My wife was not allowed to see it until after our wedding.

When I was in first or second grade, I pestered mom to make me some peanut butter cookies. "People who want to eat need to know how to cook," she said. "The recipe is on the side of the jar. I need to go help your father, so you'll have to make them yourself," she replied, and then she was gone. I didn't make the cookies but I remembered the lesson.

To watch her work is magic. She pulls ingredients from shelves without a glance. She never uses recipe books or measuring cups. One fall day when I was in sixth grade, I came home from school to see Mom making pastry crust for three apple pies. As usual, she was throwing things in the bowl with hardly a glance, all the while drinking coffee and playing cards with Dad.

"How do you do that?" I asked.

"Do what? Beat your father at rummy?" Mom said with a smile as she laid down three queens.

"No, make stuff without a recipe."

"Oh, that. Every cook memorizes the important recipes."

At my mom's insistence, I learned to cook. She really meant it when she said, "People who want to eat need to know how to cook." Let me be quick to add, however, that my skill is a dim candle and she is the sun.

Our children like to eat, so my wife and I are teaching them how to handle themselves in the kitchen. We have taught them my mom's three cooking rules. Both of them are developing their unique specialties and memorizing the important recipes.

Our Recipe

In this chapter, we will examine the specific steps of the method we overviewed in conversation four. This is our recipe for integration. I have never read a recipe book for enjoyment. I read it in order to make something. In the same way, I wrote this book and this chapter in particular, to help you make something. I suggest you weave a biblical integration lesson as you read this conversation. You will gain a greater understanding, and twice the return on your time investment, if you do each step as you read it. The method will make more sense and you will end up with a product you can use. Before reading the next paragraph, select a lesson you are planning to teach in the near future. Then, read each step and do what it says. Do not go on to the next until you have completed it.

So that the recipe is clear, uncluttered and easy to follow, I have placed the examples after the recipe rather than within it.

Follow the recipe as is, or adjust to taste.

An Overview of the Ingredients and Recipe

An overview helps us stay focused. Powerful biblical integration has three main ingredients: (1) an objective, (2) the Bible and (3) the students. Do not omit any of these from the recipe:

1. What is my objective?
2. What does the Bible say about it?
3. How does this truth connect to my students?

We prepare these three ingredients using a seven-step recipe:

1. What is my objective?
2. Which worldview category will be my focus?
3. What questions, topics and key words can I investigate?
4. What does the Bible say about my selected topic?
5. How does my topic connect to the biblical story?
6. How does my topic connect to my students?
7. How will I weave these truth threads into my lesson?

Step One: What is my objective?

Whether we use the premade objectives from our teacher's edition or create our own, biblical integration begins here. Objectives come in three sizes: small, medium and large—lesson, unit and course objectives. Any and all of these are suitable for integration.

Articulate your objective in writing.

Step Two: Which worldview category will be my focus?

Select the worldview category in which you hope to instruct your students. The purpose for this step is to bring focus to the objective. Without focus, the following steps can become overwhelming. In your first integration attempts, as you are learning the model, limit your focus to only one category. Most objectives could fit into multiple or even all six of the worldview categories. Select *one*. Think carefully about which one you will use. This sets the direction for the rest of your steps. As you become more familiar with the model, you may decide to select more than one category.

Select one of the following:
1. *God (Theology)*
2. *Reality (Metaphysics)*
3. *Humans and Community (Anthropology and Sociology)*
4. *Values and Ethics (Axiology)*
5. *Knowledge and Truth (Epistemology)*
6. *Meaning and Purpose (Teleology)*

Step Three: What specific questions, topics and keywords can I investigate?

Identify the questions, topics and key words that will help you discover the Bible's teaching on your objective and worldview category. The process is organic and often unpredictable, but generally, questions lead to topics and then topics are refined into key words.

Start by asking questions about your objective. Start wide open. Be creative, thoughtful and even humorous. Do not censor or evaluate. You can do that later. I find it helpful to speak directly to the objective. This is my favorite question to ask at this stage: "Why are you worth my time?" At this stage it is not necessary to answer all (or any) of the questions. Instead, just focus on generating as many as possible. When answers reveal themselves, ask them questions, too.

Ask your objective even more questions. Now is the time to begin to focus. Concentrate your questions on the worldview category you selected. Below, are a few of my favorite starters. Answer only the ones that relate.

How does the fulfillment of this objective help the students...
1. *Know and glorify God?*

2. *See God's creation more clearly?*
3. *Become the people God desires them to be?*
4. *Live lives of service and abundance in harmony with God's values?*
5. *Know the truth?*
6. *Discover the meaning of life and their unique purpose in it?*

Look over your questions (and answers if you have any). If you find that your best questions are in a worldview category other than the one you selected at step two, switch your focus to that category.

Use your questions to generate a list of topics. Once you have possible topics to research, identify the key words related to these topics. Find their synonyms and antonyms. Generate as many topics and key words as you can. You can be selective and evaluate later. Put diligent and creative thinking into your list. Effort at this stage will open up surprising and fruitful possibilities. Lack of effort will make forward progress difficult.

Now be selective; evaluate your work. Do not keep all the questions, topics and words on your list. Keep only those you want to research at step four. Your unused questions are not wasted. Many of them can be recycled into other parts of your lesson.

Step Four: What does the Bible say about my topics?

Use the topics and key words you generated in the previous step to help you find relevant Bible passages. As much as possible, go to the source. This means serious study and wrestling with the text of Scripture. If you have never studied the Bible in depth, ask some friends to show you how they do it. There are a number of good Bible study methods to choose from. Select the one that works best for you.

At a minimum, detailed Bible study should include the following:
1. *Making observations about the text*
2. *Asking and answering questions about it*
3. *Applying it to our contemporary situation.*

Reference works are both a blessing and a pitfall to study. They are designed to aid our study of the Bible, not replace it. Sometimes we end up glancing at Scripture and studying our resources. It should be the other way around, but having said that, we do need resources to help us.

At the risk of oversimplifying the vast array of resources available, they have three different purposes. They help us: (1) find, (2) explain or (3) summarize the content of the Bible. Concordances are the main resource for *finding* words and topics in the Bible. Commentaries, Bible dictionaries, encyclopedias, lexicons and handbooks all attempt to *explain* the meaning of a given word, topic or passage. Topical guides and theologies aim to identify and *summarize* the Bible's teachings on given themes and topics. Diligent integrators will often use all three types as they prepare.

Bible references are available in print, online and in software formats. The sheer number of resources available online makes it difficult to know where to turn. The options are always changing, but the following sites seem to be relatively stable and offer some good resources:

Biblegateway.com would be an adequate one-stop resource. It has topical guides, concordances, commentaries, dictionaries and more.

Bible.org is another good site filled with thousands of indepth articles that cover almost every passage, book and theme in the Bible.

Lumina.bible.org is bible.org's free online study suite that provides the New English Translation and brings a surprisingly rich and deep Bible study experience.

E-sword.net provides a free, user-friendly Bible study software program designed by Rick Meyers.

After you have done your homework, you will end up with more information than you can possibly use. The final part of this step is to be selective and choose the topics and teachings that are most beneficial to your students. Don't try to use it all. One or two main ideas that the students will remember are far better than ten ideas they won't.

Step Five: How does my selected topic connect to the biblical story?

At this point, we are ready to bring organization to our content. Our organizational principle is the overarching narrative structure of the Bible. The narrative plot of perfection, problem, and two-part solution of redemption and consummation, transforms a scattered list of verses into cohesive story that our students can remember. Among theologians, this exercise is referred to as biblical theology—a theological statement that follows the grand arc of the Bible's teaching from Genesis to Revelation.

Begin by articulating the original God-intended purpose of your selected topic. The first two chapters of Genesis are the richest (but not only) source for discovering this.

Describe how we distort, misuse or misunderstand the topic. We see this in the Bible from Genesis, chapter three, onwards, and in the non-biblical worldviews that confront us everywhere we turn. In the Bible, we see distortion of God's good creation expressed in two ways. First, we use it in ways that do not bring glory to God. Second, we use it in ways that detract from the abundant life God designed for His people. In the passages you use, look to include both direct statements and examples of Bible characters who illustrate the distortion. You will not need to look very far in Scripture (or the world around us) to see the misuse of God's good gifts.

Redemption and restoration are only in Jesus. Explain how the broken and distorted is redeemed and restored by Jesus' teaching, life, death and resurrection. As His redeemed people, He invites us to join Him and serve as His ambassador-agents in the redemption work. Scripture's commands to Christians all center on collaborating with God in the work of restoring all things to their proper places so that we may once again use them for His glory and our abundant living.

Finally, describe how your topic will be perfected in the consummation of all things: Christ's return.

Organize the biblical truth you discovered about your topic into the following four-point narrative:
1. *How did God intend it to be?*
2. *How do we distort, misuse or misunderstand it?*

3. *How does Jesus (in His teaching, life, death and resurrection) redeem and restore it to its God-intended purpose? How does He involve us in this work?*
4. *What will it look like when Jesus returns and brings about full restoration?*

Step Six: How does my topic connect to the students?

Real connection is the product of relationship, not formula. Know your students. The importance and value of relationship can never be overstated! As a relational teacher in authentic, loving relationship with your students, you can connect using one or more of the following three overlapping points of contact:

1. Media
2. Experiences (past, present, future and teacher created)
3. Culture and current events

The following offer some practical tips for fostering a classroom environment of relationship and connection:[8]
1. *Make your classroom a safe place for students to speak openly and honestly.*
2. *Encourage dialogue and questions. (Be prepared to answer their questions when appropriate, but note that not every question needs an answer.)*
3. *Explain WHY, not just what and how.*
4. *Help students see that the biblical worldview has the answers they hunger for.*
5. *Get below the surface. Listen to their heart, not just the words. Identify and discuss the deeper and unmentioned root assumptions that lie behind their questions.*

6. *Share and discuss quotations. Use popular media with which the students are familiar, but also include famous thinkers. Encourage students to bring in quotes they encounter.*

Step Seven: How will I weave these truth threads into my lesson?

The final step is all about weaving. It is an art form demanding an artist's eye. Everyone can learn the art, but it takes practice. Each integration carpet we weave increases our skill. Consider your first weavings as apprentice pieces showing the way toward your masterpiece.

At this point, we know our objective, our threads of biblical truth and our point of contact between them and the student. How will we pull all three together? If we fail here, our students will end up holding a tangle of yarn rather than a beautifully woven carpet.

Three sets of questions are helpful for beginning weavers:
1. *The first is easiest to answer. Where will my integration best fit into the lesson? Will it serve as an interesting opening activity? Is it a good way to wrap up the unit? Should I present it all at once, or should it come to the students bit by bit over a period of several lessons?*
2. *The second question concerns the relationship of the two contents. How will the academic subject content and the biblical integration content interact with and reinforce each other?*
3. *The third weaver's question concerns involvement. How will the students be active participants in the*

learning process? What sorts of questions will we ask them? Into what activities will we immerse our students?

These three sets of questions are not the only ones. As our skills grow, other weaving questions will present themselves and guide us into even more elaborate integration patterns.

The process of truth weaving is dynamic. Discoveries made at one step in the process may lead us to go back and revisit a previous one or cause us to jump ahead. We should not confine ourselves to a slavish observation of the steps, especially as our skills develop. For example, sometimes you may find that step two fits better after the third step, sometimes before it and sometimes it naturally answers itself somewhere in the middle.

Examples

Below are four examples. They provide snapshots of integration in science, math, literature and health. (Reviewing the worldview story example at the end of chapter two may also be helpful.)

Insect Life Cycles (Science/Biology)

1. **Objective:** Diagram and explain the life cycle of insects using essential vocabulary for both the incomplete and complete metamorphosis cycles (unit objective).

2. **Worldview Category:** Humanity

3. **Questions, Topics, Key Words:**
   a. Questions: Why do insects change so much from birth to adult? Why don't humans? What if, in our growth, we changed as much as insects do? What if humans had a complete metamorphosis? Do insects mature intellectually? Do humans mature more than just physically? What are some of the non-physical ways humans grow? Do all people develop in the same sequential cycle? Is it possible to create a "life cycle" of spiritual growth? Is salvation a sort of spiritual metamorphosis? Into what do we spiritually metamorphose?
   b. Topics: growing up, physical changes in life, the human life cycle, the spiritual life cycle, spiritual metamorphosis
   c. Key Words: growth, development, life, journey, progress, change, metamorphosis, transformation

4. **Biblical Content for Integration:** Transformation (Metamorphosis)
   a. Genesis 1.26-27
   b. Genesis 2.15
   c. Genesis 9.16
   d. Romans 12.1-2
   e. 2 Corinthians 3.18
   f. Corinthians 15.35-58
   g. Philippians 3.12

5. **Biblical Story:**
   a. Original Intention: God created us to perfectly reflect His image and likeness (Genesis 1.26-27), yet there was also to be real growth and development within that perfection (Genesis 2.15). It seems that Adam and Eve were to

develop into even greater degrees of God's likeness.

b. Distortion: Adam and Eve rebelled against God's commands and fell into sin (Genesis 3). As a result, the image and likeness of God is marred and distorted, but not erased completely (Genesis 9.16).

c. Restoration: Christ transforms us by His death on the cross. He did the transforming, not us, yet our transformation has an ongoing process of growth. Transformation happens when we submit as living sacrifices who renew their minds (Romans 12.1-2). We grow from one degree of glory to another glory (2 Corinthians 3.18).

d. Consummation: When we see Him, we will be like Him (1 John 3.2). We will have a perfected metamorphosis, but like Adam and Eve in the garden, we will (presumably) continue to grow to be even more like Christ.

6. **Students:** Give students the shared classroom experience of raising caterpillars and watching them transform into butterflies.

7. **Truth Weaving:** Focus on metamorphosis during the period in which the caterpillars are in chrysalises and as they break free. Ask the following questions to highlight spiritual transformation as the work of Christ: What are the caterpillars doing while they are in their chrysalises? (They are sleeping; they are doing nothing but allowing the changes to take place. In the same way, Christ is the one who changes us. Do not neglect to talk also about how we participate with Christ in His work of transforming us.) Emphasize the superiority of transformation by asking the following: If you had to choose between being a

butterfly or a caterpillar, which would you be? Which existence is better and more beautiful? (In the same way, a transformed life is better than anything we can imagine!)

Practical Application of Business Economics (Consumer Math/ Economics)

1. **Objective:** Apply consumer and business economic principles to real life situations (course objective).

2. **Worldview Category:** Humans and community

3. **Questions, Topics, Key Words:**
   a. Questions: What would Jesus buy? Would Jesus buy a sports car? How can I use my money to glorify God? What sort of businessperson would Jesus be? What is heaven's economy? Should Christians tithe? If we give 10%, can we do what we want with the other 90%? What is God's way to run a business? What is my responsibility toward the poor? What is the wisest way to use my money? How can I benefit God's kingdom by my profit and spending? How should I invest my profit?
   b. Topics: social justice, stewardship of resources, financial responsibility, selfishness, greed, underprivileged people in need
   c. Key Words: poor, needy, stranger, alien, invest, steward, money, giving, tithe, talent, responsibility, selfishness, greed

4. **Biblical Content for Integration:** Stewardship of financial resources
   a. Genesis 2

b. Matthew 25.14-30
c. 1 John 3.17
d. Titus 1.7-8
e. 1 Timothy 3.8
f. Proverbs 1.10-19
g. Psalm 10.3
h. Jeremiah 8.10
i. Isaiah 22.15-25

5. **Biblical Story:**
   a. Original Intention: God placed Adam and Eve in the Garden of Eden, entrusting all to their stewardship (Genesis 2). Stewardship is a way to glorify God. Matthew 25.14-30 illustrates the stewardship principle. In this parable, the master entrusts each of his servants with an amount of money. Two are good stewards who use it well, and produce a return. The other servant fails as a steward. Among other things, this story illustrates the importance of financial responsibility of the resources we have been given.
   b. Distortion: Selfishness and greed are the primary (but not only) roadblocks to godly stewardship (Psalm 10.3, Jeremiah 8.10, Proverbs 1.10-19, 1 Timothy 3.8, Titus 1.7-8). It blinds us to God and our brothers and sisters in need (see 1 John 3.17). In Isaiah 22.15-18, the steward Shebna used his position for his own gain. Cowardice and fear of failure are other reasons people do not exercise proper stewardship (see Matthew 25.14-30).
   c. Restoration: In Titus 1.7, God gives a description of a good steward. In Isaiah 22.15-18, God calls Eliakim to be a good and faithful steward. Jesus, in Matthew 16.19, refers to the Isaiah 22 passage and applies it to the apostles as faithful stewards.

d. Consummation: Matthew 25.14-30 tells us that at Christ's return, faithful stewards receive even greater authority and will enter into the joy of their Master.

6. **Students:** Create a shared experience of planning and running a small business. Give the students an additional level of ownership by allowing them to decide the product they will produce, market and sell. For example, students may decide to grow plants and sell them to other students and the community.

7. **Truth Weaving:** As the students start earning money, introduce the concept of biblical stewardship. As they learn these principles, the students can discuss how they could be good stewards of the money they earned. They may conceive a number of ideas such as class parties, saving it for their senior trip or a consumer math "fun trip", among others. (In this example, the students decided that they should not benefit from their profits. The class wanted to find a way to give the money to the underprivileged. After further student research, they decided to give farm animals through the World Vision Animal Donation Program.)

Comparing and Contrasting Works of Literature (British Literature)

1. **Objective:** Compare and contrast literature from different authors and periods (course objective), specifically applied to comparing and contrasting Canterbury Tales with Pilgrim's Progress (unit objective).

2. **Worldview Category:** Humans and Community

3. **Questions, Topics, Key Words:**
   a. Questions: Is "journey" the best metaphor for life? Can you take a journey and never leave your hometown? What does *Pilgrim's Progress* teach us about the Christian life? What does *Canterbury Tales* teach us about the Christian life? Which book gives us a truer picture of the Christian journey? Why are stories important? Are we taking life's journey alone or in community?
   b. Topics: The journey of life, living the Christian life, community, the power of stories
   c. Key Words: journey, travel, narrative, story, life, community, relationship, alone

4. **Biblical Content for Integration:** The Christian life is a journey
   a. Genesis 2.18
   b. Genesis 3.8-13
   c. Genesis 5.24
   d. Genesis 27.41-33.20 (Jacob's journey)
   e. Genesis 37-50 (Joseph's journey)
   f. Exodus-Joshua (Journey of the nation of Israel)
   g. 1 Samuel 16- 2 Samuel 24 (David's journey)
   h. Jonah 1-4
   i. Matthew 10 (The disciples' first missionary journey)
   j. Matthew 28.18-20 (The disciples' commission to go out into all the world)
   k. Acts 13-28 (Paul's missionary journeys and journey to Rome)
   l. 1 Corinthians 16.6
   m. 3 John 1.6
   n. Ephesians 2.10, 4.1, 4.17, 5.2, 5.8, 5.15
   o. 2 Peter 3.13

    p.   Revelation 3.4

    q.   Revelation 21.24

5. **Biblical Story:**

    a.   Original Intention: God made humanity perfect and designed for us to walk with Him as we live in community (Genesis 2.18, 5.24).

    b.   Distortion: Due to our sin and rebellion, we no longer desire to walk with God. Instead, we turn away and hide from our Maker (Genesis 3.8-13). As we study the life journeys of biblical characters, we see fluctuating pictures of both turning away from God and returning (Genesis 27.41-33.20, The Exodus and Jonah 1-4, among others).

    c.   Restoration: God calls us to return to Him, receive His healing and walk with him all the days of our lives. The book of Ephesians demonstrates this in its organization. The word "walk" introduces each new section in order to highlight the reality that the Christian life is a journey of walking with God (and others).

    d.   Consummation: At Christ's return, we will dwell forever with him in a new heaven and earth (2 Peter 3.13, Revelation 3.4, 21.24).

6. **Students:** Connect the concept of life as a journey with the students' travel experiences.

7. **Truth Weaving:** After reading excerpts from both books, have students write about and discuss journeys they have taken. Compare their journeys with those of *Pilgrim's Progress* and *Canterbury Tales*. Discuss the metaphor "Life is a journey." What do these books teach us about the reality of the Christian journey? Small groups can read and describe the

journeys of biblical characters, and compare them to *Pilgrim's Progress* and *Canterbury Tales*. End the unit with a study of Ephesians' instructions on how to "walk" life's journey.

Reproductive Cycle and Sexual Education (Middle School Health)

1. **Objective:** The students will understand and explain the reproductive cycle and human sexuality in order that they may make healthy life choices (unit objective).

2. **Worldview Category:** Humanity

3. **Questions, Topics, Key Words:**
   a. Questions: Why are so many people (students and teachers) afraid to talk about sex? Is sex education the responsibility of the school, the parents, the church, or all three? Is it possible to teach sex education in a way that is not awkward and uncomfortable? How can we teach biblical truth about sex in a powerful way? How can we combat the world's view of sex? How can we present an attractive alternative to the world's view of sex?
   b. Topics: marriage and family, sexual misconduct, sexual purity, consequences of sex outside of marriage, puberty, resisting the world's temptations
   c. Key Words: sex, lust, adultery, fornication, purity, temptation, marriage, obedience

4. **Biblical Content for Integration:** God's designs for human sexual expression within the bounds of marriage, sexual purity
    a. Genesis 1.27-28
    b. Genesis 2.20-25
    c. Exodus 20.14
    d. Proverbs 6.32
    e. Matthew 5.27-28
    f. Proverbs 11.6
    g. 2 Peter 2.7-10
    h. 1 Corinthians 6.11
    i. Ephesians 5.3
    j. Colossians 3.5
    k. 1 Thessalonians 4.7
    l. Hebrews 13.4
    m. 1 John 4.17
    n. Matthew 22.30

5. **Biblical Story:**
    a. Original Intention: God created males and females equal but different (Genesis 1.27). Sex is good; it is part of God's plan for people (Genesis 1.28), but only within the bounds of marriage. God's perfect plan for marriage is one man and one woman together for life (Genesis 2.20-25).
    b. Distortion: Sex is distorted whenever it is practiced outside the bounds of marriage (Exodus 20.14, Proverbs 6.32, Matthew 5.27-28, Proverbs 11.6, and Ephesians 4.19). All around us, in music, movies, TV and even our friends tell us that sex outside of marriage is okay. Doing things God's way is uncommon, but God can give us the resolve to stand strong (2 Peter 2.7-10).
    c. Restoration: Regardless of our past (1 Corinthians 6.11), God calls us to sexual purity now (Ephesians 5.3, Colossians 3.5, 1

Thessalonians 4.7). Marriage is a good gift given by God (Hebrews 13.4).

   d. Consummation: In the resurrection our love is perfected (1 John 4.17) and we are in perfect relationship with each other, yet there is no marriage (and presumably, no sex) Matthew 22.30.

6. **Students:** Create a shared classroom experience of raising guppies.

7. **Truth Weaving:** Set up a number of small aquariums in the classroom with several pairs of guppies in each. Do this about a month before the unit is scheduled to begin. Have students take the responsibility of caring for the guppies (feeding, cleaning the aquariums, etc...). Once the guppies begin to have babies, teach the reproductive cycle of guppies. After receiving parent permission, transition into the human sexuality lesson by discussing the similarities and differences between guppies and humans. Students may identify some of the following: Humans and guppies are similar in that they both have males and females. Males and females have different appearances. They are different because guppies do not get married. They do not love each other. They do not take care of their babies. The tagline for the purity lessons can be "You're not a guppy!" This memorable line can give the students a simple statement to remind them that God's plans for human sexuality and marriage are different from His designs for animals.

Conversation 6: Methodology and Biblical Integration

Opposite Ends of the Spectrum

Early in our careers, God called my wife and me into international teaching. Answering the call was one of the best decisions we ever made. As we prepared to go to South Korea, our organization had us take a battery of personality tests. One test measured whether we preferred a structured, schedule-driven approach to life or a spontaneous, flexible, "keep our options open" outlook. My wife scored all the way on the scheduled, organized end of the spectrum, while I was completely on the other side. We could not have been further apart. The results were not a surprise.

Our advisor, who was helping us prepare for the transition, discussed the test results with us. As he looked at them, he said, "I've never seen a couple with such radical differences in this category. I think you should know that this might cause some tension in your relationship."

We had only been married for two years but were well aware of the differences. We looked at each other and laughed. "Yes, we know," I said. "It's come up once or twice in the last couple of years."

Now, after eighteen years of marriage, I am still aware of those differences and I appreciate them more than I can say. God, in His wisdom, made us different and brought us together.

Diversity Working in Unity

Heterogeneity is God's plan. Diversity working in unity is the structure of nearly everything in the universe. It is certainly the structure of His body, the church. If all His people were the same, we would never be able to do everything He has called us to do (1 Corinthians 12.14-23).

We can draw a teaching application from this truth. There is not a single "right way" to teach. Any number of people could take the same content and teach a great lesson, yet no two of them would teach it in the exact same way. My wife is an excellent teacher, one of the best I have ever encountered, but she teaches very differently than I do. She teaches according to her personality and I teach according to mine.

Personality shapes how we teach, and rightly so. That does not mean, however, that personality differences can become an excuse for sloppy teaching methods. Methodology is not an "anything goes" endeavor. In fact, it is so important that we should keep the following maxim in mind:

HOW we teach is (nearly) as important as WHAT we teach.

What is your reaction to this idea? The first time I encountered it, I was not so sure I agreed, but as time has gone by, I have become more and more convinced that the statement is true. At this point, I think that I might even remove the word "(nearly)." The "how" is as important as the "what."

Biblical integration is both a science and an art. We cannot ignore either of these. As a science, integration has objective truth content that we discover and integrate using a given method. We are all integrating the same biblical truth. We do not teach our own private religion, but rather we teach "the faith that was once for all delivered to the saints." (Jude 1.3).

Biblical integration is also an art. As an art, each act of integration is a creative attempt to ensure that we weave the biblical worldview into the students' lives. Even when two teachers use the same method, the results are different. We each have a distinct methodological style. Rather than suppress this we should rejoice in it.

Methodology: The Product of Our Personality and Our Philosophy

Our methodology matters. It determines HOW we weave the biblical worldview into our lessons. Our methodology is a product of our personality and our philosophy.

Removing Our Masks

Our personality is a huge factor on our teaching style. We are each a unique, one of a kind image of God. Each of us reflects Him in an unrepeatable way. We are "fearfully and wonderfully made" (Psalm 139.14)!

Since this is true, be yourself. You reflect God in a way no one else can. Let your portrait of God shine.

"Who are you?" the Caterpillar in Wonderland asked Alice.
"I hardly know, sir," she replied.

We may feel like Alice. How do we find ourselves? The answer is surprising and counterintuitive. It explains why so many people fail at the task. We do not find ourselves by focusing on ourselves. In Matthew 16.24-25, Jesus taught that we find ourselves when we deny ourselves and follow Him. When we do this, we discover who we are and can become the unique image God designed us to be.[9]

Often as teachers, we put on a mask and pretend to be someone else. This does a disservice to God and His kingdom. He wants our unique image to shine. Wearing a mask is frustrating, stressful and exhausting. The distance between the mask, and who we really are, determines the amount of exhaustion, stress and frustration we feel in life and in the classroom. God calls us to remove our masks and be who He created us to be.[10] Refusing to do so is to work against our Creator.

We need to drop our masks and be ourselves in life and in the classroom. When we do, we will have a less exhausted, less stressful, and more enjoyable teaching experience.

An art gallery where every painting is the same would be dull. Much of modern education tries to reduce teaching to this. Our unique teaching methodology is a painting style. Some teachers are impressionist, others surrealist. Some are abstract, modern or renaissance. Which one are you?

Do not change your style. Instead, celebrate it. Whichever it is, perfect it, and develop it so that you are doing your absolute best work within the style that is your own.

Knowing Our Problem and Purpose

Methodology is also a product of our philosophy. At the risk of being too simplistic, a teacher bases their philosophy on their answers to two interrelated questions. Our answers reveal our philosophy:

1. *What is the primary human problem?*
2. *What is the primary task or purpose of a teacher?*

The first identifies what is wrong. Is our problem ignorance? Is it lack of resources, or sin, or alienation, or fear, or broken relationship? Maybe it is a combination of these, or something else entirely. We all have an answer we operate from, even if we cannot articulate it.

The second addresses what we do to help our students overcome the problem. Is the teacher's task to give knowledge, teach morality, or prepare the student for a career? Maybe the task is to help students think for themselves or achieve self-actualization. Maybe the task is something else completely.

Methodology Lessons from the Master Teacher

Jesus is the perfect teacher. Rabbi, or teacher, is one of the most common titles given to Him in the gospels. Both His friends and enemies used it when addressing

Him. Of course, He was much more than just a teacher, but all will agree that He was a teacher.

Even though His culture and "classrooms" were different from ours, we have much to learn from Jesus, our Master Teacher.

His methodology lessons fill the gospels, but we will focus on three: (1) Jesus was relational, (2) His method generated intellectual engagement, and (3) He taught the whole person. How a teacher applies these three lessons will depend upon their personality and philosophy-based teaching style, but teachers who desire to emulate Christ *will* apply them.

Relational Teaching

Jesus was relational. In each encounter, He recognized the uniqueness of the person and addressed each as an individual. Education should occur within the context of relationship. The opening chapters of Proverbs are a good example of this biblical concept. Educational institutions should not be like factories. Instead, we can build learning communities in our classrooms. We are successful in this when each student can and does express their unique perspectives and questions. This requires us to allow them to have some voice and choice in their learning.

Relational education requires an atmosphere of love and respect. At a minimum, we demonstrate love through two actions. First, we are to treat people the way we wish to be treated. Second, we commit to listen to others. In a real community, we hear everyone's voice. We need to model these rules, and insist that our students observe them at all times. When we do, relational education will flourish.

Intellectually Engaging Teaching

Not only was Jesus relational, He was also intellectually engaging. This can be a challenge to achieve. Most of us are relational *or* intellectual; rarely does the ability to do both come naturally to us. We should strengthen whichever is our weaker area.

Our methodology should lead the students to intense, serious thinking and intellectual interaction with the content, regardless of what they believe. They should not feel forced or "brainwashed" to believe the same as the teacher. Instead, we should challenge students to know what they believe and be able to explain why. Our integration should cultivate an environment that encourages both seeking and belief! Sometimes this is a difficult balance.

Jesus engaged people by: (1) asking questions, (2) telling parables and (3) living out His message. One of my education professors told me that Jesus' ratio of questions to answers was two questions to every one answer. She followed that statement up (appropriately) with a question, "What does that tell us about teaching?"

Jesus also engaged people by telling stories. Every teacher should be a good storyteller. Educationally affective stories are related stories. Jesus' parables brought light because they connected truth to real life and compared the unknown with the known.

Finally, Jesus engaged people as a role model. He exemplified His teaching. He was a living illustration. His lifestyle caused people to ask questions. Among many possible examples, consider that the disciples asked Jesus to teach them to pray after they observed His prayer life (Luke 11.1). We must live out the biblical worldview.

There is a litmus test to see if we are being intellectually engaging. *Are the students wrestling with the content and coming to know what they believe?* There are two opposing problems to avoid. We do not want our students to be "force fed" the answers. We also do not want them to fail to come to conclusions.

Holistic Teaching

Jesus also taught the whole person. This is the third methodology lesson we learn from the Master Teacher. His teaching was for the heart, mind and hands. It was never just content for the mind! The heart and its values are within the domain of education. Students need both direct teaching and modeling of values.

The head and heart need an outlet. Our students must be taught to act on what they learn. We need to teach them skills so that they can actively engage the world and do the work of the kingdom. In our age of informational overload, thinking skills are especially important.

How do we know if we have successfully taught the whole person? We can apply Jesus' litmus test. *Are the students experiencing real transformation?* If they are, then we know that our teaching has permeated their heads, hearts and hands.

These three methodology lessons of relational, engaging and holistic teaching are just the beginning. Study Jesus' teaching methods in the Gospels. The book of John is a good place to begin because in it we see some amazing one-on-one relational teaching interactions.

Conversation 7: Integration for Non-Christian Students

Lions, Ghosts, Doppelgangers and Succubi

Charles Williams was a most unusual Christian novelist. His stories are set in the modern world (of the early twentieth century), yet peopled with archetypal lions, ghosts, doppelgangers, succubi and even an evil necromancer. The novels are profound and rich in symbolism and spiritual truths.

Williams' works invite comparison with those of C. S. Lewis. The two men were close friends and shared membership in the literary club *The Inklings*. Both used the vehicle of fantasy to present biblical truth, and both are popular with Christians and those who are not. The two novelists understood how to communicate. Their winsome narratives draw people in, even those who do not want to be drawn.

We need to learn from them. As Christian educators, we have a responsibility to integrate the Bible. This responsibility is to all our students, Christian and non-Christian alike.

The issue of biblical integration for non-Christian students is an important one. As we navigate this complex and complicated issue, there are two factors to consider, first, the non-Christian student, and second, how the school environment affects our integration.

First, consider the student. We all have non-Christians in our classrooms. Everything we have previously said about knowing the students and having a relationship with them applies here. Knowing them includes knowing where they stand in their spiritual lives. Is the boy in the back left corner an atheist, an adherent to another religion or a disgruntled child of a pastor? What about the quiet girl in the second row? What is her attitude toward Christ? Is she ignorant of Him or has she made a conscious decision to reject Him? Is that difficult student interested, or apathetic, or hostile? Each attitude requires a different approach, but the Spirit uses relationship and genuine care to begin to prepare hearts for the seeds of truth. He calls us to integrate for each of them, even the outspoken antagonistic ones. The apostle Paul was such a person before his conversion.

Biblical Integration for Non-Christians in Christian Schools

In Christian schools, the administration encourages the teacher to integrate. Some students are eager and thankful for the opportunity to learn the Bible, but others are not so receptive. In such instances, the classroom is a living example of the story of the sower. We have a room full of hearts that represent all the soil types mentioned in the parable.

We can decide simply to scatter the seed, but with a little extra effort, we can prepare the soil so there is a greater chance for germination. Biblical integration in such situations is working the soil. It is preparation for evangelism.

Each student is a potential garden for God's seeds of truth. We have learned from Jesus that teaching is to be holistic. The work of soil preparation takes place on all three fronts: (1) the heart, (2) the head and (3) the hands.

The Heart

We all have a heart-hunger for God and His truth, beauty and goodness. Our deepest longing is to know God and be known by Him. As Augustine said, speaking to God, "You have made us for Yourself and our hearts are restless until they find their rest in You." Winsome integration shows unbelievers that Jesus fulfills their deepest heart longings, and satisfies their desire for truth, beauty and goodness. It is our duty to show our non-Christian students that the biblical worldview satisfies their heart's hunger.

The Head

God created our minds with a desire to know, understand and make sense of the world we experience. The Biblical worldview answers our questions and gives us a paradigm for further inquiry. We should view biblical integration as a special form of apologetics. Our integration should demonstrate to the non-Christian student that the biblical worldview makes sense. It allows us to understand the world we live in. Its explanation fits the data empirically, internally, and logically.

"Why should I learn about the biblical worldview? I have absolutely no intention to become a Christian. I don't believe that it satisfies my longings and desires. I don't think it even offers a very good explanation of reality." I have heard a number of students make these sorts of comments. In such situations, I politely disagree with them, and then give two secondary reasons for knowing the biblical worldview. Of course, the primarily reason we integrate the Bible is for God's glory and the student's well-being, but these other secondary reasons are also true and valid.

First, knowing the biblical worldview allows the individual to be a more understanding world citizen. Christianity is the largest religion in the world. About one third of the world self-identifies as Christian. If we want to understand our global community, we need to understand Christianity. In order for this reason to carry weight, we also need to have a place in our curriculum for teaching other popular worldviews.

Another reason unbelievers need to know the biblical worldview concerns art, literature and culture. A friend of mine went to Hawaii to learn how to teach an *Advanced Placement* literature course. During the session, one of the participants asked the instructor an important question, "What's one thing I can do to help my students get higher scores on the final exam?"

"Teach them the Bible," was his immediate reply. The room was silent. It was not an expected answer. He explained. "Almost all of the great intellectual works of the Western world assume knowledge of the Bible and Christianity. Without understanding the allusions they cannot appreciate or interpret the work of art."

There are more than just those two secondary reasons, but these are the two that I give. They have satisfied every student or parent who has ever asked me. Use these reasons or others, but the important thing is to be prepared to give reasons for non-Christians to know the biblical worldview.

The Hands

Action is the third area in which we can prepare the students to be receptive to God's truth. They want to see that Christian belief makes a difference in a person's life, that it affects their actions. They know we are Christians, so they take note of how we act. Our actions can turn heart-soil rocky and hard or soften it so that it is prepared to receive the seeds of truth. Many students come to Christ because of the actions of a godly teacher. We need to exemplify Christ all day, every day. (First period Monday morning is always my hardest.)

Students also want to know that Christian belief can guide their own actions. They want to do something meaningful and lasting. We need to show them that the biblical worldview gives them a reason for engaging in our world. We need to help them see that it provides a basis for social justice, care of the environment and all sorts of other important actions. It gives them a purpose to live for and direction for life's actions.

Biblical Integration in Public Schools

Christian teachers in public and non-Christian schools are in a different situation. Should they integrate the Bible? This is an important question. Even though it is conceivable that the only Christian in the room would be the teacher, my answer is "yes."

Our model works equally well in any school situation, and most of the ideas mentioned above apply to students in public schools, too. The non-Christian school environment, however, requires a different attitude. The Christian teacher in such a situation is an undercover subversive who is working for the good of others. The picture I have in mind is the French resistance fighters during the Nazi occupation.

A whole book could (and should) be written about this, but here I highlight just one important thought. Do not sound a trumpet to announce your good deeds. Jesus reprimanded the religious hypocrites for showing their acts of righteousness to the world. Biblical integration is a good deed. It can lead students to Christ, who is their heart's desire, and give them an abundant life. Weave your integration seamlessly into your lesson. Do it quietly and respectfully. Do not be abrasive or combative.

His Spirit, Not Our Power

Teachers have great power. We should never abuse our position or authority. We should never force students to make decisions they are not ready to make. We collaborate with the Spirit. We must not try to usurp His work.

We cannot be obnoxious, offensive telemarketers who just will not give up. The gospel is offensive, and several times the Bible repeats this reminder (Romans 9.33, 1 Peter 2.8), but we need to make sure that the offense is with the gospel and not with the messenger. In everything remember, one person sows, another waters, but God is the one who causes the growth (1 Corinthians 3.6-8).

Pray these requests from Colossians 4.3-6.

> [T]hat God may open to us a door for the word, to declare the mystery of Christ... that I may make it clear... Walk in wisdom toward outsiders, making the best use of the time. Let your speech always be gracious, seasoned with salt, so that you may know how you ought to answer each person.

A Concluding Thought

Yavas, Yavas

After seven wonderful years in Korea, God called my wife and I (now with two children) to teach in the country of Turkey. We boarded the plane with trepidation. Korea had become home, but now we were moving to a country we had never even visited.

We touched down in the height of Turkish summer. The Ankara airport was chaos. We were sweaty and dusty as we hauled six hundred and thirty pounds of luggage off a creaking, ancient carousel and wrestled it onto carts. All the while, we tried (unsuccessfully) to keep our two small children, aged two and five, from getting into mischief.

Dripping and weary we exited the baggage claim and stepped into a cacophony. We were looking for a Serdar Bay, the Turkish man who had agreed to pick us up. The flurry of activity overwhelmed us. We feared we had missed him because our flight had arrived late. Then we spotted our name card. The man holding it beamed when we made eye contact and waved.

"Merhaba! Nasilsiniz?" I greeted him with the only two Turkish words I knew. His smile grew, and he kissed me on both cheeks in typical Turkish greeting.

He took hold of my wife's luggage cart and let loose a flood of Turkish. I didn't understand a word. He read the look of panic on my face and switched to English. "Oh, by your greeting, I thought you knew Turkish."

"I'm sorry to say that those are the only two words I know," I confessed. "I hope to learn, but I don't know anything yet."

"Yavas, yavas," he said with a smile. "It means slowly, slowly. There's no rush, you'll learn." As the days and weeks went by, I heard those words daily. In Turkey, the expression works in almost every situation.

It is a good motto to use for biblical integration. I hope that you are eager to integrate the Bible into the subject and lives of your students, but remember Serdar Bey's advice. Start slowly. Trying to do too much, too fast, usually brings failure and frustration. The result of these is reluctance to try again.

The ideal is seamless biblical integration woven into every lesson, but this is an unrealistic goal, especially at the start. Begin by thinking of biblical integration in terms of units. Start by planning one powerful biblical integration lesson for one unit in one class. Over time, slowly work up to one biblical integration lesson woven into each unit of each class. As time goes by and you become an experienced weaver, you may be able to do even more.

Do not expect perfection right away. "If a thing is worth doing, it is worth doing badly," G. K. Chesterton famously remarked. Sometimes the only way to move forward is by stumbling. Watch a toddler and you will see that this is true.

I pray that God would kindle within you a passion and vision for biblical integration. May He continually feed that fire through all your years of teaching. I pray that your integration would train your students to think and act biblically so that each can live an abundant life for the glory of God.

Appendix

Worldview Examination

As a biblical integrator, you are seeking to weave the biblical worldview into the subject and lives of students. But in order to do so, you must be certain the worldview you are weaving is, in fact, the biblical one. You can only do this if your own worldview is in order. Proper care for it requires you to ask yourself two questions, one descriptive, the other prescriptive. The descriptive question is, "What is my worldview?" The prescriptive question asks, "Is my worldview biblical?"

You can answer the descriptive question by articulating your beliefs in the six worldview categories:

1. God
2. Reality
3. Humanity and Society
4. Ethics, Morality and Value
5. Knowledge, Truth and Thinking
6. Meaning and Purpose

The questions below will help you identify your worldview. Try to give brief, yet complete answers. Answer according to your actual beliefs, not the beliefs you think you should hold. If you are not sure if you really believe what you claim, ask yourself this question, "How have my recent actions demonstrated this belief?" Real belief always expresses itself.

God

1. *Who is God?*
2. *What is God's character-nature?*
3. *Who is Jesus?*
4. *How would you describe God's relationship with humans?*
5. *How would you describe God's relationship with the universe and what occurs in it?*

Reality

1. *How would you describe the world we live in?*
2. *How did the universe come into existence?*

Humanity

1. *What is the major barrier to joy, peace, satisfaction, and happiness in life?*
2. *What are the defining characteristics of a human being?*
3. *How does one have a relationship with God?*
4. *What is humanity's task and place in the universe?*
5. *What obligations does a person have toward others?*
6. *What does a good community look like?*
7. *What are the biggest problems in your community?*
8. *What is the most effective way to bring social change?*

Ethics, Morality and Values

1. *What is goodness?*
2. *What is beauty? What things are beautiful?*
3. *What is valuable? (Rank your top five to ten values)*
4. *How do you know right from wrong?*
5. *Is there a standard or basis for good behavior? What is it?*
6. *What does it mean to be a good person?*
7. *What ought (should) a person do?*
8. *How can you be good?*
9. *What motivates you to do the right thing in difficult circumstances?*

Knowledge, Truth and Thinking

1. *What is truth?*
2. *What is faith? What is knowledge? What is the relationship of the two?*
3. *Why is it possible to have accurate knowledge?*
4. *How do you know what is true?*
5. *How do you demonstrate that your knowledge is true?*

Meaning and Purpose

1. *What is the meaning of human history?*
2. *How does a person find their meaning and purpose?*
3. *What gives your life meaning and purpose?*
4. *How is your meaning and purpose tied to your beliefs?*

Teaching

1. *What is the purpose of education?*
2. *What are the distinctive traits of a Christian teacher?*
3. *If you could teach your students only one thing this year, what would it be?*

Addendum

1. *What are some of your other important beliefs?*

The Prescriptive Question

Once you have identified your current worldview, you can ask yourself the prescriptive question, "Is my worldview biblical?" In other words, are your beliefs in the six worldview categories in harmony with God's word? Hold up your answers to the light of Scripture. The best way to do this is by studying the Bible one book at a time. Immerse yourself in God's word. Let His Spirit teach you. Seek to relate the Bible to the truth claims you encounter in science, entertainment, philosophy, advertising, psychology, the arts and everything else.

Constantly examine your worldview to confirm that only truth grows in it. Unbiblical beliefs spring up like weeds. Tending your worldview requires weeding and constant nourishment from the Bible.

All of Scripture should shape your worldview, but the following books and passages are an especially good place to begin:

> *The Gospel of Matthew*
> *The Gospel of John*
> *Ephesians*
> *1 John*
> *Romans*
> *Isaiah 40-66*

With Gratitude

I end with a heartfelt thank you to the many people who have made the content and writing of this book possible. Your personal and intellectual investments have enriched my life. Thank you, first to Yoshi for encouraging me to write this and listening as I did so. You have helped me in innumerable ways on this book and in life. Words cannot express how much you mean to me. Solon and Megumi, thank you for bringing so much joy to my life. Mom and Dad, you are the wisest people I know, and I aspire to be like you. Thank you for a lifetime of love and support. Lora, your editorial expertise has made this book better than I ever could have made it on my own. Thank you for investing in this book!

I owe a debt of gratitude to all the many teachers and professors who have shared their wisdom with me over the years, some in person and others through their writings. Pastor Collins, Chris Miller, James Grier, Ronald H. Nash, Alistair McGrath and Peter Kreeft are chief among many. Thank you. My writing echoes with your words.

About the Author

D. P. Johnson is a full time teacher and international church and conference speaker. He has taught students in every grade from prekindergarten through high school, and has spoken in nine different countries on three continents. Currently, he teaches high school philosophy and worldview formation courses at an international school in Asia. He has been weaving biblical integration lessons for nineteen years.

D. P. Johnson completed his undergraduate studies in Bible, science and education at Cedarville University and earned a Masters of Religious Education (MRE) and a Masters of Arts in Interdisciplinary Studies (MA) from Asia Biblical Theological Seminary of Cornerstone University.

When not in the classroom, he enjoys cross-country running, art and studying theology, philosophy and ancient cultures. He also enjoys traveling with his wife and two children. Together, they recently completed a backpacking trip across Tibet. In the future, they hope to hike the Inca Trail to Machu Picchu in Peru and the *Camino de Santiago* in Spain.

Notes

[1] In the Bible, listening cannot be divorced from obedience.

[2] Francis Schaffer, *A Christian Manifesto* (Crossway, 2005), p 17.

[3] Learn more about this organization at www.new-eyes.

[4] Ed Stetzer, *Barna: How Many Have a Biblical Worldview?* http://www.christianitytoday.com/edstetzer/2009/march/barna-how-many-have-biblical-worldview.html accessed July 21, 2010. (Read about the details of this survey (and others) at www.barna.org.)

[5] Sigmund Freud, *New Introductory Lectures on Psycho-Analysis* (W. W. Norton & Company, 1990), p 195-96.

[6] I base this ordering and organization of worldview on the teaching and books of Ronald H. Nash. See especially his introduction to philosophy, *Life's Ultimate Questions* (Zondervan, 1999).

[7] I am indebted to Alistair McGrath's excellent apologetics book, *Intellectuals Don't Need God (and Other Modern Myths)* (Zondervan, 1993) for many of the ideas in this section.

[8] Once again, I am indebted to Alistair McGrath's excellent apologetics book, *Intellectuals Don't Need God (and Other Modern Myths)* (Zondervan, 1993) for many of the ideas in this section.

[9] I owe this insight to the writings and teachings of David Brenner. See especially the book *The Gift of Being Yourself* (InterVarsity Press, 2004).

[10] I am indebted to the book *Truefaced* by Bill Thrall, Bruce McNicol and John Lynch (NavPress, 2004).

Made in the USA
Las Vegas, NV
13 October 2022